Introduction

Welcome to a simple little resource that will bring you hours of fun. Every dad in the world knows that his daughter spells love, T-I-M-E. And because we know this is true, we do our best to spend time with her whenever we can. But have you ever been short of things to do once you're together?

This book is filled with things you can do with your precious daughter. Many of them can be done in a short time, and very few will cost you more than you spent on this book! But I can promise you that the investment you make in your girl will reap lifelong dividends.

God bless you and don't forget . . . have lots and lots of fun.

Your friend,

[signature: Robert Wolgemuth]

And God said,
"Let the water teem with living creatures, and let birds fly
above the earth across the expanse of the sky."
God made the wild animals according to their kinds,
the livestock according to their kinds,
and all the creatures that move along
the ground according to their kinds.
And God saw that it was good.

GENESIS 1:20, 25

Wild Kingdom

Go on a nature walk in a local park or forest preserve.

Take along books for identifying flowers, trees, and birds.

Take magnifying glasses and binoculars to get a closer look.

Start lists of all the varieties you see. (Start these lists on your trip.

But just for the fun of it, keep the lists going.)

"Give, and it will be given to you.
A good measure, pressed down, shaken together
and running over, will be poured into your lap.
For with the measure you use, it will be measured to you."

LUKE 6:38

The Dollar Game

Go on an excursion to a big discount store like Woolworth's,
Wal-Mart, or K-Mart. Give your daughter a dollar, and you take a dollar.
Tell her that she can spend it on anything she wants. You do the same.
Stay together as you make your selections. As you're leaving the store
and you pass the photo booth, invest in some funny face photos of you
and your daughter together. Since most of these booths take four
different shots, be happy, sad, silly, or monsterish for each picture.

I will instruct you and teach you
in the way you should go;
I will counsel you and watch over you.

PSALM 32:8

The Safari

Get a map from a local real estate broker and plan an outing for
new experiences in your own community. Decide together what
you would like to do, and then map out your route with a highlighter.
Instead of driving in the car, you might consider going by bicycle,
city bus, train, or foot. Wear a backpack with your lunch
packed inside and carry your camera for lots of pictures.

The house of the righteous contains great treasure.

PROVERBS 15:6

Collector's Items

Help your daughter start a collection. Ask around for ideas. You'll be amazed
at what people collect—silver charms, stamps, miniature figurines,
tea cups, golf balls, spoons, teddy bears, match boxes, butterflies, etc.
You get the idea. Encourage her to start a collection of her own,
then let her decide what to collect. Now you have just solved
one of the biggest problems facing daddies everywhere:
"What should I get my daughter for her birthday, Valentine's Day,
or when I'm coming home from a long business trip?"

But the eyes of the LORD are on those who fear him,
on those whose hope is in his unfailing love.

PSALM 33:18

Did You See That?

Go to ordinary places and watch things together. Visit an airport to see
the planes take off, an observation deck of a tall building to see how
little the ant-sized people look below, or a construction site with
gargantuan trucks in action. The conversation and questions
will make this a memorable and creative experience.

God's signature is on the whole of nature.
All creatures are love letters from God to us.
They are outbursts of love, set in creation by God,
who is love, to kindle the fire of love in us.

ERNESTO CARDENAL

Sketch It

Give your daughter a blank book for drawing what she sees.
Suggest that she record some of your activities together by drawing them.
The book will be a treasured keepsake of her times with you, and
she'll enjoy her "primitive art" when she looks back on her
drawings of birds, trees, leaves, animals, and—of course—Daddy.

Then God said,
"Let the land produce vegetation: seed-bearing
plants and trees on the land that bear fruit
with seed in it, according to their various kinds."
And it was so. . . .
And God saw that is was good.

GENESIS 1:11–12

Planting a Memory

Take your daughter to a local nursery and pick out a tree. Choose one that changes leaves every season like a maple or an oak. Plant the tree together, and watch it grow as she grows. Take a picture of her in front of the tree on birthdays and other special occasions. By the time she leaves for college, you'll be amazed at how tall the tree has grown!

"For I know the plans I have for you,"
declares the LORD,
"plans to prosper you and not to harm you,
plans to give you hope and a future."

JEREMIAH 29:11

Mysterious Journey

Girls of all ages love guessing games. Invent a "mystery outing."
Tell your girl how to dress and what to bring, but don't tell her where
you're going. You can provide clues and hints so she will try to guess where
you're headed. It doesn't have to be Disneyland or SeaWorld to be special.
She will be surprised and pleased when you reach the park, picnic table,
mall, or woodland path that you've chosen for the mystery trip.

When I set God at the center of my life,
I realize vast freedoms and surprising spontaneities.
When I center my life in my own will,
my freedom diminishes markedly.

E U G E N E P E T E R S O N

Hoop It Up

Keep a basketball in the trunk of your car. (You may want to keep it
in a box to prevent it from rolling around when you turn every corner.)
When your daughter is with you and you pass by a public park or
school that has basketball goals, stop and shoot a few hoops.
Play "Horse" or a little one-on-one. If she's still small, put her on
your shoulders and let her shoot from there. She'll love the spontaneity,
and you'll love feeling like the tallest man in the world! (To her you will be.)

He called out to them, "Friends, haven't you any fish?"
"No," they answered.
He said, "Throw your net on the right side
of the boat and you will find some."
When they did, they were unable to haul
the net in because of the large number of fish.

JOHN 21:5-6

Cast Away

Take your daughter fishing. What better place is there to relax and talk? Show
her how to bait the hook. You don't need a boat for this activity.
You can stand on the bank of a nearby river, pond, or creek.
What's important here isn't how many fish you catch;
it's the time together that counts.

Honest scales and balances are from the L<small>ORD</small>;
all the weights in the bag are of his making.

P R O V E R B S 1 6 : 1 1

A Not-So-Dumbbell!

Include your small daughter in your workout—not as a coworker, as a free weight! Let her sit on your shoulders while you do push-ups. Or if that's a little too challenging, hold out your arm in the flexed position and let her do chin-ups on it. You'll be amazed at how many giggles this evokes!

It takes a long time to become young.

PABLO PICASSO

Batteries Not Included

Take time to teach your girl some of the games from your own childhood like marbles, hopscotch, foursquare, jacks, pick-up sticks, or Chinese checkers. Be sure to tell stories of how you used to play these games as you are sharing the fun of each "oldie."

Life in the presence of God should be
enjoyed every moment of every day.

A.W. TOZER

No Thanks, We're Just Looking

Visit a pet store or aquatic center near your home.
Explain that you are not going to buy anything but
that you would like to say "hello" to all the furry and scaly
creatures that are staying at the store. If your girl enjoys walking
in the mall as one of her activities, it makes the experience
much more fun if a pet store stop is included on the schedule.

So I commend the enjoyment of life,
because nothing is better for a man under
the sun than to eat and drink and be glad.
Then joy will accompany him in his work all the
days of the life God has given him under the sun.

ECCLESIASTES 8:15

My Little Wheel-Washer

Washing the car in the driveway doesn't have to be done all alone.

Why not let your girl enjoy the outdoors with you?

Give her a steel wool pad and a brush to clean the wheels, or

if she's a toddler, give her a bucket of water and a paintbrush.

Let her create water pictures on the driveway.

Be sure to notice them before they dry!

The LORD our God, the LORD is one. Love the LORD your God with all your heart and with all your soul and with all your strength. These commandments that I give you today are to be upon your hearts. Impress them on your children. Talk about them. . . . Tie them as symbols on your hands. . . . Write them on the doorframes of your houses and on your gates.

DEUTERONOMY 6:4-9

Pick a Letter

A favorite thinking game is "Letter-Up." You name a letter,
B for instance, and tell your girl to find five things in the room
that begin with that letter. Say, "Go!" and time her.
If she's kindergarten age, she will want to blurt out each one as
she sees it. If she's old enough to write, let her save all five
and give them to you on paper. Why not have her
collect things that begin with the letters in her name?

That everyone may eat and drink,
and find satisfaction in all his toil—
this is the gift of God.

ECCLESIASTES 3:13

International House of Daddy

Have pancakes for breakfast. Daddy can cook them and
form initials with the batter. Since you're giving
Mom the morning off, this can make Saturday
or Sunday morning something special.

T o be able to enjoy one's past is to live twice.

MARTIAL

Hollywood Here We Come

Help your girl produce her own video. These make great keepsakes or gifts for distant relatives and friends. You and your daughter can make up news broadcasts about the current affairs at your house, commercials with products you enjoy using, and interviews with favorite toys and dolls. You can also create music videos out of your favorite songs. Be sure to make yourself a copy of this production. It will provide laughs and enjoyment in a few short years, as the kids see themselves when they were younger.

And let us consider one another
in order to stir up love and good works,
not forsaking the assembling of ourselves together.

HEBREWS 10:24–25 NKJV

The Special Plate

Designate a one-of-a-kind dinner plate that you call the "special plate."
Use it for your daughter—or another member of your family—
whom you want to honor on an ordinary night. When it's on the table,
everyone will applaud the person for the good deed, thoughtful word spoken,
a wise choice they made, or some kind of special accomplishment.

Keep on loving each other as brothers.
Do not forget to entertain strangers,
for by so doing some people have
entertained angels without knowing it.

HEBREWS 13:1–2

Will You Be Mine?

Adopt a "grandmother" or "grandfather" with whom your family can share holidays, notes, visits, and meals. You can find these treasured friends in your neighborhood, in a local nursing home, or through your church.

The benefit to your daughter of this cross-generational love far outweighs the time and effort it takes to make the phone calls and trips, take the flowers, or write the notes. These new friends have lots of wisdom, experience, and love beneath that white hair.

Ask and it will be given to you;
seek and you will find;
knock and the door will be opened to you.
For everyone who asks receives; he who seeks finds;
and to him who knocks, the door will be opened.

MATTHEW 7:7-8

Craw-Daddy

If you feel adventurous and you live near a clean creek, take your daughter "crawdad hunting." Wade into the creek (make sure you wear tennis shoes) and look under big rocks for crayfish. It's just scary enough to be fun! You may even want to pick one up for her, holding it behind its pinchers, of course, and let her watch it wriggle. Then release it into the water and watch it scurry away in a dusty blur. This is a great time to discover what kinds of animals live in the water right near you. It's fun and a great way to learn.

I will lie down and sleep in peace,
for you alone, O LORD, make me dwell in safety.

PSALM 4:8

Slumber Party Nap

Take a family nap on the living room floor on a Sunday afternoon.
Be sure to take the phone off the hook and have a fan on for
"white noise" in the background so the first person to awaken can
quietly leave the room without disturbing the other nappers.

They had with them every wild animal according
to its kind, all livestock according to their kinds,
every creature that moves along the ground
according to its kind and every bird
according to its kind, everything with wings.
Pairs of all creatures that have the breath of life
in them came to Noah and entered the ark.

GENESIS 7:14-15

Daddy's Ark

Get out a box of crayons. Both you and your daughter
draw a picture of the kind of animal that is most like you.
It helps to have a picture book of animals nearby to look at for ideas.
You may even give suggestions to younger girls to point out that the
hippopotamus likes to play in the water, or the deer is graceful
and shy, or the koala bear is cuddly and likes to climb trees.
When you're finished, show each other your drawings
and talk about the traits of your chosen animal.

47

Let all things be done decently and in order.

1 CORINTHIANS 14:40 NKJV

Clean-Up Olympics

Playing games when it's time to clean up helps

lighten the load and the clutter in your home.

"Let's see who can pick up the most toys in five minutes!"

"You pick up the green and yellow things, and I'll get the red and blue ones."

"The blocks have to go to bed now. Next, you need to tuck in all the animals.

That doll is so sleepy. Put her in her bed."

You'll also get rave reviews from your wife who

will notice your light touch and inventive spirit.

Humor is the great thing.
The minute it crops up, all our
irritations and resentments slip away,
and a sunny spirit takes their place.

MARK TWAIN

Hey, Look This Way!

Distraction is one of the best ways to take advantage of a small child's
short attention span and to guide her away from undesired activities.
When your toddler heads for the dangerous or breakable or inedible object,
make a silly noise like a choo-choo train or use a crazy voice (if you can
learn to do the Donald Duck quack, it will go a long way) until you
can move the object out of sight. Being creative in replacing that forbidden
object can be a challenge. Pick her up and dance with her in your arms
and keep exploring for a new, acceptable object she can play with.

I must say that I find television very educational.
The minute somebody turns it on,
I go to the library and read a book.

GROUCHO MARX

Turn It Off; Read a Book

The minutes with your girl in your lap or next to you in a chair reading
will create relationship-enhancing memories. If she's old enough, select
a book that she can read to you. Show her how important books are to
you by helping her create a cozy reading corner in her room or somewhere
else in the house. A little lamp on a pedestal next to a fluffy
pillow on the floor can be her special, private reading corner.
A trip to the library or her favorite bookstore with Daddy
can add to the pleasure and ensure hours of reading adventure.

I *will lie down and sleep in peace,*
for you alone, O LORD,
make me dwell in safety.

PSALM 4:8

Camp Daddy

Living room camping can bring the spirit of adventure into the safety
of your own home with nothing more than a sheet, a few blankets, some
beach towels, and flashlights. Your girl will remember this with delight.
Throw the sheet over a table or chairs arranged in tent fashion. Give everyone
a "sleeping bag," beach towel, and flashlight. Turn out the room lights
and eat hot dogs, marshmallows, graham crackers, and chocolate kisses.
Tell adventure stories, read a book by flashlight, and talk about your
favorite trip when you were a boy. Toddlers and preschoolers
will love hanging out and camping with Daddy.

May the favor of the Lord our God rest upon us;
establish the work of our hands for us.

PSALM 90:17

Another Day at the Office

If you work at an office, pick up your daughter from school and take her back with you on a Friday afternoon. (Be sure to clear this visit with your supervisor first.) Give her a calculator and a list of numbers to add. Let her spin in a swivel chair, make confetti with the hole-puncher, and make necklaces and "crowns" by hooking paper clips together. Ask her to draw a picture for you to remind you of her day at the office.

Let them praise his name with dancing
and make music to him with tambourine and harp.
For the LORD takes delight in his people;
he crowns the humble with salvation.

PSALM 149:3-4

May I Have This Dance?

If your daughter is in middle school or older, take ballroom dancing lessons together. Often you can find these lessons offered at a local YMCA or community center for a reasonable price. It will be fun for you both and a great investment in her future. If she finds herself at a ball or formal dance later, she won't have to be nervous because she doesn't know how to dance.

She'll waltz in and out of social settings with ease!

For the kingdom of God is not
a matter of eating and drinking,
but of righteousness, peace and joy in the Holy Spirit,
because anyone who serves Christ in this
way is pleasing to God and approved by men.

ROMANS 14:17-18

Let's Do Lunch

If your daughter is in kindergarten, first, or second grade,
surprise her by showing up at school for lunch one day. Eat with her
in the cafeteria. If she's older, you might want to take her somewhere
off-campus for lunch. (As crazy as it may seem, sometimes
older girls are embarrassed to be seen eating with dear old dad!
Don't worry, though. They'll eventually grow out of it.)

How fair is your love,
My sister, my spouse!
How much better than wine is your love,
And the scent of your perfumes than all spices!
How fair and how pleasant you are,
O love, with your delights!

SONG OF SOLOMON 4:10, 7:6 NKJV

I Love Your Mother

When your girl starts dating, write her a letter about
how you met her mother. Give juicy details about how she looked,
what you loved about her, and what qualities showed you that her
mother was the one for you. Include pictures of some of your earlier dates!
She'll be amazed at the fact that you remember so much, and it
may open a doorway for future conversations about her dating life.

Listen . . . to a father's instruction;
pay attention and gain understanding.

PROVERB 4:1

How-To

Go to the library and check out some how-to books.
Pick a subject that's new for both of you—building
birdhouses, gardening, even cooking! Select a simple project
and practice following instructions together. This will help
your daughter learn to follow instructions in other settings, too.

The heavens declare the glory of God;
the skies proclaim the work of his hands.

PSALM 19:1

Dad the Tour Guide

Take your daughter on a tour of the city where you live.
Point out the historic sites, the fire station, the tallest buildings,
and the most unique houses. Show her places where you
have special memories, or drive down the curviest road
in the area. Let the trip last fifteen to thirty minutes, and
make your last stop somewhere that sells ice cream or milkshakes!

You need three things in the theatre—
the play, the actors and the audience,
and each must give something.

KENNETH HAIGH

Tickets, Please

Have a show for the family. Let your daughter
pick a song to sing or dance to, or if she's more of
an actress, let her dress up and perform a dramatic monologue!
Make tickets out of construction paper together, and make popcorn
for the audience. Then invite the other members of the family to the
theater/living room. You can be the usher, and your daughter can be the star!

A *merry heart does good, like medicine,*
But a broken spirit dries the bones.

PROVERBS 17:22 NKJV

Hug You Very Much

Make up special hugs. Give each other a "seal hug"—
hug like usual but pretend your stiffened forearms are flippers, and
clap each other on the back like a seal might do. For a "crab hug,"
start on opposite ends of the room and walk sideways until you
reach each other, then hug as usual. Make sure you laugh a lot as you
traverse the room! Or try a monster hug like Frankenstein must have
done with his daughter. These make for great inside jokes later. One person
announces, "Crab hug!" and the other one has to quickly jump into action.

Behold, how good and how pleasant it is
For brethren to dwell together in unity!

PSALM 133:1 NKJV

Family Jeopardy

Play a family trivia game after dinner one night.
Write down questions like, "What's your brother's
favorite movie?" and "Where did your mother and I meet?"
Let M&M's™, Skittles™, or Starburst™ candies be the prizes.
Have a bonus round or a lightening round for a bigger
prize like a trip to the zoo or an afternoon at the movies.

I will offer to You the sacrifice of thanksgiving,
And will call upon the name of the LORD.

PSALM 116:17 NKJV

Thanks a Lot

In the month before Thanksgiving, help your girl make a "Thankful Box."
Take a shoebox and cover it with decorative paper. Cut a three-inch slit in
the top, and tape a pencil on a string and a note pad to the top of the box.
Every night after dinner or before bedtime prayer, ask everyone in the family
to write down something that they're thankful for. At Thanksgiving dinner,
open the box and read all the "little things" your family recorded.

Don't forget to thank your daughter publicly for the beautiful box!

Therefore, my beloved brethren, be steadfast, immovable, always abounding in the work of the Lord, knowing that your labor is not in vain in the Lord.

1 CORINTHIANS 15:58 NKJV

A Regular Appointment

Schedule regular times with your daughter. Pick any night of the week or
weekend, and let her know that every week at this time will be daddy/daughter
time. She'll know that every Saturday afternoon from 2:00 to 4:00
she can count on the two of you doing something together. The time span
doesn't have to be long, just consistent. This will help her feel secure,
and it will help you get to know your daughter like you never have before!

Teaching us that, denying ungodliness and
worldly lusts, we should live soberly,
righteously, and godly in the present age.

The Coupon Clipper

Teach your daughter to be a savvy shopper. Go through
the Sunday paper together and look through all the coupons.
Cut out the ones that look like something your family would enjoy,
then go to the grocery store with your girl. See how much money
you can save. You may want to designate a special project for
this saved money—maybe a child sponsorship organization.

F_{or} God is not a God of disorder but of peace.

1 CORINTHIANS 14:33

Making the Dishes Disappear

Even chores like evening kitchen clean up can be made into
a daddy-daughter game. After dinner, tell your girl to close her eyes
as you remove one thing from the table. She has to guess what you took,
then it's her turn to remove something while you are not watching.

Before you know it, the food is put away, the dishes have been
cleared, and you have a happy helper. Mom will especially like this game!

Let us love one another,
for love comes from God.
Everyone who loves has been born of God
and knows God.

1 JOHN 4:7

Squeeze Play

Take your daughter's hand and tenderly squeeze it four times in a row.
Then, she squeezes your hand three times. You return the three squeezes
with two of your own. She ends the silent "conversation" with one
final strong squeeze of your hand. The interpretation of this conversation is:

"Do you love me?" Four words, four squeezes. Her answer is,

"Yes, I do." Three words, three squeezes. Your response is,

"How much?" Two words, two squeezes. And her final answer

comes in a strong squeeze. No interpretation necessary.

B*ecause of the Lord's great love we are*
not consumed, for his compassions never fail.
They are new every morning;
great is your faithfulness.

LAMENTATIONS 3:22,23

Daddy's Wake-Up Call

Rethink your daughter's wake-up routine, especially
one special day a week. For me, Sunday is the easiest. Welcome
your child into the day with a gentle backrub or a silly song, like
"You Are My Sunshine." She will begin to look forward to the special
morning when Daddy begins her day with a tender wake-up routine.

${F}$athers, do not exasperate your children; instead,
bring them up in the training and instruction of the Lord.

EPHESIANS 6:4

Your Happy Face

Hunting for a "happy face" can be turned into a sport with Daddy.
This really works well with a young girl who is bored or whining.
Act like you are trying to find something very important.
Lift up chair cushions, look behind doors, and open boxes,
while calling out, "I wonder where it is?" Ask your girl to
help you find her happy face, and laugh when you find your
own happy face. When she smiles, say, "There it is, I see a smile!"

"Be strong and of good courage,
do not fear nor be afraid of them;
for the LORD your God,
He is the One who goes with you.
He will not leave you nor forsake you."

DEUTERONOMY 31:6 NKJV

What If?

Some games can be a mental challenge as well as
a helpful teaching tool to prepare your daughter for emergency situations.
"What would you do if you were at the mall and became separated from me?"
"If you were on a walk by yourself and saw a snake, what should you do?"
"You are home all by yourself and the electricity goes off.
Would you know what to do?"
The list of "what ifs" can be endless and can prompt stories of your
own childhood solutions. Remember not to scare your girl but to keep
scenarios light and fun. Reassure her that God always protects us, and
that one way to be safe is to know what to do if certain things happen.
This will boost her confidence in herself—and her faith in God.

This is the day the LORD has made;
let us rejoice and be glad in it.

PSALM 118:24

Heaven in the Morning

Get up early enough some morning to watch a sunrise with your daughter.
It may be difficult to coax her up at 5:30, but promise her that the colors
will be worth it. As the sun slowly rises, each moment will build into a
"Wow!" moment that will assure your girl that you were not exaggerating.
Be sure to say, "Honey, remember what this looks like; always remember."
She will be able to close her eyes anytime and bring back the memory
of her dad and the small corner of heaven she saw with you.

Awake, north wind,
and come, south wind!
Blow on my garden,
that its fragrance may spread abroad.

SONG OF SONGS 4:16

The Sniff Test

Conduct a fragrance test. Gather a few simple objects:
a flower or herb from the garden, a bar of soap, a piece of cookie,
coffee, a bottle of cologne, hand creme, shampoo, or chocolate.
Put a blindfold on your girl and have her guess the object you
waft past her nose. She will be anxious to play the game back to you.

Parents lend children their
experience and a vicarious memory;
children endow their parents with a vicarious immortality.

GEORGE SANTAYANA

Create a Book Together

Write down a story as you and your girl make it up.
Take turns with sentences or thoughts. When you have finished,
you may set it aside for a couple of days. Then edit it together
when your ideas are fresh. Let your girl illustrate the pages and
make a cover and title page. Let her make a cover for your book
with wrapping paper or old wallpaper. Start your library of
"Classics by Daddy & Me" when your girl is small.

Who takes the child by the hand,
takes the mother by the heart.

DANISH PROVERB

Better than "Store-Bought"

Make a love note for Mom. List the reasons
you and your girl love her, write her a poem,
and draw pictures. Put lipstick on you daughter's lips
(she'll like this) and let her kiss all over white paper.
Be creative, and this handmade card will be
more special than one you could buy.

How beautiful on the mountains
are the feet of those who bring good news,
who proclaim peace,
who bring good tidings, who proclaim salvation.

ISAIAH 52:7

My Favorite Thing Today

Have a family "Good News Report" at dinner or just
before bedtime. Ask your daughter what the best part of her day was,
then tell her your good news. It may be that you were in the garden
and a hummingbird flew by. Or you may have seen your dream car
on the freeway. Let her learn from you to focus on her blessings,
and to enjoy the gifts all around her.

For as the soil makes the sprout come up
and a garden causes seeds to grow,
so the Sovereign LORD will make righteousness
and praise spring up before all nations.

ISAIAH 61:11

Planting Memories

Get a few packets of seeds in the spring and leave them
with a note on your daughter's dresser. Tell her that you would like
to plant the seeds on the weekend when you and she will have
a garden date. The anticipation of spending time with you and the
brightly colored packets will be promises of joy to come.

Therefore, as God's chosen people, holy and dearly loved, clothe yourselves with compassion, kindness, humility, gentleness and patience.

COLOSSIANS 3:12

Share a Grateful Heart

Have a watch with a second hand on it and tell your girl that she has
thirty seconds to think of someone who has shown a special love for her.
Tell her to think of someone who let her know that she really mattered.
Let her share her thoughts with you. Remind her that she can be
a person who will be someone else's "special encourager" by
doing small things like giving a big smile or a compliment.

I*f* you fully obey the LORD your God
and carefully follow all his commands I give you today,
the LORD your God will set you
high above all the nations on earth.
All these blessings will come upon you and accompany you
if you obey the LORD your God.

DEUTERONOMY 28:1–2

Share the Wealth

Help your daughter count her blessings on a car trip.
Look at the speedometer or the clock, and choose a number.
For example, if you choose the number five, have your girl
mention five things that she is thankful for. Of course,
she needs to hear your list, too. Counting blessings is
a fun way to encourage both of you to have a happy heart.

For so He gives His beloved sleep.

Behold, children are a heritage from the LORD.

PSALM 127:2–3 NKJV

Round-Trip Kisses

A special bedtime kiss can be the best part of getting ready to fall asleep.

After prayers, lean over and kiss your daughter's left cheek and say, "Daddy loves you." Then kiss her right cheek and say, "Mommy loves you." Lastly, kiss her forehead and say, "God loves you." Finish the sequence with, "Good night, precious girl." She'll fall asleep feeling secure and loved.

E*ven the sparrow has found a home,*
and the swallow a nest for herself,
where she may have her young—

Feathered Friends

Make a small bird sanctuary. Buy some good birdseed at your local grocery or garden store. Put the seed in a flat dish, set it in plain view of a window, and watch the neighborhood birds visit. Help your daughter identify the birds by keeping a bird picture book nearby. Let her keep a list of the birds that come to see you. You may also want to purchase a clock that chimes the hour with different bird songs. Place it near your viewing window. The chiming will beckon her to see if any visitors have come.

May the favor of the Lord our God rest upon us;
establish the work of our hands for us—
yes, establish the work of our hands.

PSALM 90:17

Bike Wash

Have a bike wash together. Make sure winter-stored bikes
are in good condition; check the tires, and let your daughter
oil any squeaks. Then go on a bike ride with your girl.

Nothing in life is trivial.
Life is whole wherever and whenever we touch it
and one moment or event is not less sacred than another.

VIMALA THAKAR

State Plate Fun

On a car trip, look for different state license plates.
Have your daughter keep a running list of all the ones she sees.
These games can help increase your girl's awareness of
what's around her and may make the miles speed by faster.

The one who sows to please the Spirit,
from the Spirit will reap eternal life.
Let us not become weary in doing good,
for at the proper time we will reap
a harvest if we do not give up.

GALATIANS 6:8-9

Mission Statement

Create a family mission statement that spells out your vision and values.
Explain to your family the importance of talking about your vision and
values and having them written down. What makes our family unique?
What are our goals? How do we want to act toward each other?
How can we treat others? This allows her to enter into an activity
that helps her identify with your work and your values at home.

All Scripture is God-breathed
and is useful for teaching, rebuking, correcting
and training in righteousness.

2 TIMOTHY 3:16

Memorize a Bible Verse Together

Choose a verse and reference and write it down on a card.
Have your daughter do the same. Set a goal for memorizing it together.
Agree to meet on the day you choose and say the verse out loud
to each other. Build a repertoire of shared verses and give her a file box
to store her cards. A good one to start with is Philippians 1:3,
"I thank my God every time I remember you."

"Or suppose a woman has ten silver coins and loses one.
Does she not light a lamp, sweep the house
and search carefully until she finds it?
And when she finds it,
she calls her friends and neighbors together and says,
'Rejoice with me; I have found my lost coin.'"

LUKE 15:8-9

Twenty Quarters

Tell your girl to look for quarters and save them
for a special fun night out with dad. When she has twenty quarters,
take her to an arcade and play skee-ball until the quarters
are gone. Then treat her to a frozen yogurt on the way home.

For the LORD your God will bless you
in all your harvest and in all the work of your hands,
and your joy will be complete.

DEUTERONOMY 16:15

Family Portrait

Ask your daughter to draw a picture of your family.
Let her use crayons, construction paper or whatever tools she chooses.
Have her sign her name and date it. Take it to a frame shop,
have it matted and framed, and hang it in your office.
She'll be thrilled to see it there!

I *thank my God every time I remember you.*
He who began a good work in you
will carry it on to completion
until the day of Christ Jesus.

PHILIPPIANS 1:3,6

Lunch Bag Surprise

When you leave for a trip, leave several lunch bags
in her room with a number on each bag to coincide with
how many days are left until you return. Put something in
each one to remind your daughter that you are thinking of her.
A piece of candy, an "I love you" note, a postcard,
a dollar, or an assignment to draw a picture
for you can make her feel close when you are gone.

He will yet fill your mouth with laughter
and your lips with shouts of joy.

JOB 8:21

Mail from Daddy

Draw a cartoon or cut a joke from a magazine or the newspaper,
and send it to school in your daughter's lunchbag or mail it to her
from work. She will smile and know that you are a fun daddy to live with.

Sing to him a new song;
play skillfully, and shout for joy.

PSALM 33:3

Singing While You Work

While doing chores, add a song. Teach your daughter
how to whistle if she is young. A favorite to sing is
"I've Been Working on the Railroad" while you rake leaves or
wash the car together. It makes the task so much more fun,
and you will be creating a memory too!

My mouth will speak words of wisdom;
the utterance from my heart will give understanding.

PSALM 49:3

Word Power

Introduce a new vocabulary word occasionally at dinner.
Ask your daughter if she can work the
word-of-the-day into the conversation.

One of the most common mistakes
in prayer is to keep to a system
or a posture or a resolution for
no other reason than it once worked.
If it does not work now, give it up and try another one.

HUBERT VAN ZELLER

Please Pass the Squeeze

Hold hands and pass a squeeze around
the table before the mealtime prayer.

Make room for that which is capable of
rejoicing, enlarging, or calming the heart.

GERHARDT TERSTEEGEN

Special Delivery

Write a letter to your daughter on her birthday or Christmas.

Tell her what events you thought were special during

the year and praise her for her accomplishments.

This will take a little time, but it will be well worth it.

Over the years, she'll save these treasured letters from her daddy.

Indeed the L ORD gave Job
twice as much as he had before.

Surprise Gift

Sometimes it's hard to know what she wants.

So take your daughter shopping and ask her to pick out something
that she'd especially like to give to her mom, her sister, or a friend.

Buy it while you're together that day. Take it home and wrap it
with her name on the package. Won't she be surprised when
she opens the package and discovers the treasure inside is for her!

And over all these virtues put on love,
which binds them all together in perfect unity.

COLOSSIANS 3:14

Place Mat Fun

Give your daughter pieces of construction paper
to match the number of people in your family. Ask her
to draw pictures and make a special place mat for each person
with their name on it and pictures that remind your girl of that person.
Surprise Mom by having them on the table and by setting the table, too.
This way, you win points with your wife and your daughter!

And now these three remain: faith, hope and love.
But the greatest of these is love.

1 CORINTHIANS 13:13

The Ol' One, Two, Three

Before you leave for work, write three notes that say
"I Love You" to your daughter. Put one in her backpack,
one in her lunch box, and one on the kitchen counter
for her to see at breakfast. Tell her she is Daddy's precious girl.

Then he touched their eyes and said,
"According to your faith will it be done to you";
and their sight was restored.

MATTHEW 9:29-30

I   S e e   S o m e t h i n g   Y o u   D o n ' t   S e e

Play "Bee Bee Bumblebee, I see something you don't see, and it is red."

Choose a color, and pick an object in the room of that same color.

Don't tell her what the object is. Give her three guesses to pick

the object you see. Tell her when she's "warm," "cold," or

"really hot" to help her find it. When she guesses it,

then it's her turn to let you guess an object of her choice.

[C]hildren] are a heritage from the Lord,
children a reward from him.
Blessed is the man whose quiver is full of them.

PSALM 127:3,5

Shamrock Hunt

Search your yard for a four-leaf clover together.
Tell her four-leaf clovers represent good luck, and you're
the luckiest daddy in the world to have her for a daughter.

There are toys for all ages.

Piles o' Fun

Rake a huge pile of leaves together and jump into them
with your daughter. Then, before they're all over the yard again,
have her hold the bag open while you stuff the leaves in.
Then make another pile of leaves and do it all over again.

He put a new song in my mouth,
a hymn of praise to our God.
Many will see and fear and put their trust in the LORD.

PSALM 40:3

Name That Tune

Play "Name That Tune" with your girl. Hum a tune like
"Row, Row, Row Your Boat" or "You Are My Sunshine."
Pick a more contemporary song if she's older.
When she guesses the tune, she gets to hum a song for you.

Let them give thanks to the LORD for his unfailing love
and his wonderful deeds for men,
for he satisfies the thirsty
and fills the hungry with good things.

PSALM 107:8-9

How Now, Brown Cow

Make "brown cows" (root beer floats) with your daughter.
Put a scoop of vanilla ice cream in the bottom of two tall glasses.
Tell her to pour root beer or cola over the ice cream,
and watch the fizz bubble up to the top of the glass.
Sing the "cow" verse of "Old MacDonald Had a Farm,"
then drink the treat and laugh.

A wise man's heart guides his mouth,
and his lips promote instruction.

PROVERBS 16:23

Silly Spelling

This is a great game for when your daughter brings home one
of those spelling or vocabulary lists. Weave each word on her list
into a story about a family vacation, a fictional adventure,
or a description of your girl. The story is fun, and it
will help her learn how to use and spell the words, too!

"No eye has seen,
no ear has heard,
no mind has conceived
what God has prepared
for those who love him"—
but God has revealed it to us by his Spirit.

I CORINTHIANS 2:9-10

Marvelous Journey

Take a coin, and make up a story for your girl
about the life of the coin. Imagine who first owned it,
what happened to it from there, and how it eventually came to you!
This will encourage her imagination and provide fun for you both.

He who has daughters is always a shepherd.

SPANISH PROVERB

It's Showtime

Read a Bible story to your daughter, then act it out with her.
Let her pick which character she'd like to be and
which character she'd like you to be. Use household items
as props. A red blanket could be the Red Sea, a spatula
could be a queen's scepter, a stuffed animal can be a sheep,
and a baby blanket secured with a scarf makes the
perfect headdress for lots of Bible characters.

We always thank God, the Father of our Lord Jesus Christ,
when we pray for you . . .
that you may live a life worthy of the Lord
and may please him in every way:
bearing fruit in every good work, growing
in the knowledge of God, being strengthened
with all power according to his glorious might.

COLOSSIANS 1:3, 10-11

Prayer Board

Make a prayer board for your home.

A cork bulletin board will be perfect for your daughter's room,
or for a more central location like the refrigerator, magnets work well.
Each week, add a new picture of someone you can pray for together.

Every night pray for those on your prayer board, thanking God
for them and asking Him to bless them in specific areas of their lives!